Little Rabbit Foo Foo

RE-PLAYED BY
VIVIAN FRENCH

FROM THE BOOK BY
MICHAEL ROSEN AND ARTHUR ROBINS

WALKER BOOKS
AND SUBSIDIARIES
LONDON · BOSTON · SYDNEY

First published 2000 by Walker Books Ltd
87 Vauxhall Walk, London SE11 5HJ

2 4 6 8 10 9 7 5 3 1

Playscript © 2000 Vivian French
Original text © 1990 Michael Rosen
Illustrations © 1990 Arthur Robins

This book has been typeset in ITC Highlander.

Printed in Singapore

British Library Cataloguing in Publication Data
A catalogue record for this book is
available from the British Library.

ISBN 0-7445-6726-2

Notes for Children

Little Rabbit Foo Foo is the story of a very BAD rabbit
and a very GOOD fairy.
You may know the story already, but it doesn't
matter if you don't.

This book is a little different from other picture books.
You will be sharing it with other people and telling
the story together.

You can read

this line

this line

this line

or this line.

Even when someone else is reading, try to follow the words.
It will help when it's your turn!

We know a story.

Would you like to hear it?

Yes!

Yes!

Tell us the story.

Tell us now!

Little Rabbit Foo Foo –

Little Rabbit who who?

Little Rabbit Foo Foo

Riding through the forest –

What was he riding?

Riding a motorbike.

Was he riding fast?

Yes, very very fast.

Very very very fast?

Very very VERY fast!

Tell us the story.

We'd better start again.

Little Rabbit Foo Foo

Riding through the forest –

B'rrm! B'rrm! B'rrm!

B'RRM! B'RRM! B'RRM!

Scooping up the field mice –

What did he scoop them with?

He scooped them with a net.

Was it a big net?

Yes, it was a big net.

A very very big net?

A very VERY big net.

Tell us the story.

We'd better start again.

Little Rabbit Foo Foo

Riding through the forest –

B'rrm! B'rrm! B'rrm!

B'RRM! B'RRM! B'RRM!

Scooping up the field mice –

Swish! Swish! Swish!

SWISH! SWISH! SWISH!

And bopping them on the head.

Bop! Bop! Bop!

BOP! BOP! BOP!

What did he bop them with?

He bopped them with a hammer.

Was it a big one?

Yes, a very big one.

That's not nice.

Not nice at all.

Bop! Bop! Bop!

EEK! EEK! EEK!

Poor little field mice.

What happened next?

Shhh! And we'll tell you.

Down came the Good Fairy.

Who?

The Good Fairy.

How do you know she was good?

Because she helped the field mice.

Was she very very good?

Very very VERY good.

What did she do?

She said, "Little Rabbit Foo Foo,

I don't like your attitude,

Scooping up the field mice –

Swish! Swish! Swish!

SWISH! SWISH! SWISH!

And bopping them on the head."

Bop! Bop! Bop!

BOP! BOP! BOP!

Eek! Eek! Eek!

EEK! EEK! EEK!

What else did the fairy say?

The Good Fairy.

The very Good Fairy.

The very very very Good Fairy.

The Good Fairy said,

"I'm going to give you three chances to change,

And if you don't,

I'm going to turn you into a goonie."

What's a goonie?

Something nasty.

Something very nasty.

Something horrible!

OOOOOOOOOOOOOH!

What happened next?

Little Rabbit Foo Foo

Riding through the forest –

B'rrm! B'rrm! B'rrm!

B'RRM! B'RRM! B'RRM!

Scooping up the wriggly worms –

Swish! Swish! Swish!

SWISH! SWISH! SWISH!

And bopping them on the head.

Bop! Bop! Bop!

BOP! BOP! BOP!

Just a minute!

What is it?

What noise do worms make?

Ow! Ow! Ow!

OW! OW! OW!

Oh. Are you sure?

Quite sure.

Down came the Good Fairy.

Did she look after wriggly worms, too?

She looked after everything.

Because she was a very Good Fairy.

A very very very Good Fairy.

And she said,

"Little Rabbit Foo Foo,

I don't like your attitude,

Scooping up the wriggly worms –

Swish! Swish! Swish!

And bopping them on the head."

Bop! Bop! Bop!

Ow! Ow! Ow!

And the Good Fairy said,

"You've got two chances to change,

And if you don't,

I'm going to turn you into a goonie."

OOOOOOOOOOOOOOH!

We know what comes next.

Bet you don't!

Bet we do!

What is it, then?

Little Rabbit Foo Foo

Riding through the forest –

B'rrm! B'rrm! B'rrm!

Scooping up the tigers –

Swish! Swish! Swish!

And bopping them on the head.

Bop! Bop! Bop!

Growl! Growl! Growl!

GROWL! GROWL! GROWL!

Down came the Good Fairy

And she said,

"Little Rabbit Foo Foo,

I don't like your attitude,

Scooping up the tigers –

Swish! Swish! Swish!

And bopping them on the head."

Bop! Bop! Bop!

Growl! Growl! Growl!

"You've got one chance left to change,

And if you don't,

I'm going to turn you into a goonie."

OOOOOOOOOOOOOH!

He's only got one chance left.

One last chance.

Or he'll be a goonie.

Little Rabbit Foo Foo –

Hey! It's my turn.

But I want to say it.

I know how to do it.

Can't I have a go?

Let's take turns.

Little Rabbit Foo Foo

Riding through the forest –

B'rrm! B'rrm! B'rrm!

Scooping up the goblins –

Swish! Swish! Swish!

And bopping them on the head.

Bop!

Bop!

Bop!

BOP!

Oof!

Oof!

Oof!

OOF!

Down came the Good Fairy

And she said,

"Little Rabbit Foo Foo,

I don't like your attitude,

Scooping up the goblins –

Swish! Swish! Swish!

And bopping them on the head."

Bop! Bop! Bop!

Oof! Oof! Oof!

"You've got no chances left,

So I'm going to turn you

Into a GOONIE!"

POW!

So the mice and the worms

And the tigers and the goblins

All lived happily ever after.

Notes for Teachers

Story Plays are written and presented in a way that encourages children to read aloud together. They are dramatic versions of memorable and exciting stories, told in strongly patterned language which gives children the chance to practise at a vital stage of their reading development. Sharing stories in this way makes reading an active and enjoyable process, and one that draws in even the reticent reader.

The story is told by four different voices, divided into four colours so that each child can easily read his or her part. The blue line is for more experienced readers; the red line for less experienced readers. When there are more than four children in a group, there is an ideal opportunity for paired reading. Partnering a more experienced reader with a less experienced one can be very supportive and provides a learning experience for both children.

Story Plays encourage children to share in the reading of a whole text in a collaborative and interactive way. This makes them perfect for group and guided reading activities. Children will find they need to pay close attention to the print and punctuation, and to use the meaning of the whole story in order to read it with expression and a real sense of voice.

The Big Book version can be used to introduce children to *Story Plays* in shared reading sessions. The class can be divided into groups to take part in reading the text aloud together, creating a lively performance.